WOLF TREE

WOLF TREE

Alison Calder

Edited by Elizabeth Philips.
Cover and book design by Duncan Campbell.

Cover image: "Yellow Tree in Blue Forest," by Julio Lopez Saguar, Photonica Collection/Getty Images

Printed and bound in Canada at Marquis Book Printing.

Library and Archives Canada Cataloguing in Publication

Calder, Alison C. (Alison Claire), 1969-
    Wolf tree / Alison Calder.

Poems.
ISBN 978-1-55050-359-3

I. Title.
PS8605.A455W64 2007   C811'.6   C2007-901257-4

1   2   3   4   5   6   7   8   9   10

2517 Victoria Ave.
Regina, Saskatchewan
Canada   S4P 0T2

Available in Canada and the US from:
Fitzhenry & Whiteside
195 Allstate Parkway
Markham, Ontario
Canada   L3R 4T8

The publisher gratefully acknowledges the financial assistance of the Saskatchewan Arts Board, the Canada Council for the Arts, the Government of Canada through the Book Publishing Industry Development Program (BPIDIP), Association for the Export of Canadian Books, the Government of Saskatchewan, through the Cultural Industries Development Fund, and the City of Regina Arts Commission, for its publishing program.

 Canada Council   Conseil des Arts
for the Arts   du Canada

 SASKATCHEWAN
ARTS BOARD

Canadä

 Regina
CITY OF REGINA
Regina Arts Commission

For Warren

contents

<u>S O O T E R K I N</u>

GRAVITY

WOLSELEY

SEXING THE PRAIRIE

SOOTERKIN

When I was small a bird
flew into my eye.
At first, wings battered,
heart beating the sound
a handful of pebbles
dropped from a bridge into water.
I covered my face, looked away
from others.
They were confused by fluttering
behind my eyes, scratching sounds.
When I cried pinfeathers smothered the sun.

Lately I've learned to see through wings.
My eyes become golden, my fingers
turned talon. I seek high places.
One day soon I'll climb higher than you
can imagine. I've told no one my plan.
Only the corner of my eye can give me away.
A small fluttering thing tries to get out.

SOOTERKIN, MY TWIN

"Dr. John Maubray…believed that Dutch women were disposed to bring forth an evil-looking little animal, which they called de suyger *or* sooterkin… *The sooterkin sucked all the infant's nourishment, like a leech, and the child was dead and dessicated when it was born in such unpleasant company. Dr. Maubray even claimed that he had seen and delivered a sooterkin…" –* FROM *A Cabinet of Medical Curiosities* BY JAN BONDESON

sooterkin, my twin
how oft I see you in dark corners of this room
so like our early home, a hot dark womb
the stove that bade us rise like bread
from our undreaming sleep

when our mother bore us
into this bright place
we shrieked to be returned
and when the blood-smell weakened
I ope'd my eye to spy your figure gone
and none remarking

my baby's mouth then had no tongue
to say that you had been

the rat inside my crib, the kitten found
on my frail chest, I knew that you yet were
and still I had no tongue

and though I grew
I grew not fat, a pale reed-girl
and hollow, o
my dark sister
       I see you by the fire
       I see you by the stair

our cord yet binds us

a clot upon the bedclothes, the mark
upon my breast of four small teeth

I think you have a thing of mine
I am coming to call it back

In the glass display case, the two-headed calf
looks left, looks right. Faces
only a mother could love.
Four eyes. Two noses.
White stars on each forehead,
matching cowlicks.

This jar, a fetal pig. Bulbous eyes
slate-coloured. Rubbery baby
about to bawl, snout hidden
by tiny trotters, awash
in a constellation of matter.

Freaks. And these four legs,
this narrow neck, would never hold
their weight. Mistakes.
So what hand
spilt this milk, what tongue
licked these stars?

ZIP (UNTITLED)

The joke with Zip was this:
he thought he ran the show.
He'd mimic Ringling, smoking a cigar
and shouting orders from the sideshow stage.
He'd strut, and fire the other freaks.
The rubes and Ringling laughed,
they knew who was boss.
When Zip tossed back the change
crowds threw him in performance
they said it proved him stupid

and so they bought more tickets.

Before Zip died he opened his eyes, said
well, we sure fooled 'em for a long time.
Zip the nondescript, stupid pinhead Zip
pulling his shaggy suit over everybody's eyes.

PLATE NO. 47 (ZIP: PINHEAD, C. 1885)

The following year a celebrated incident gave Zip an additional name. The Prince of Wales (later Edward VII) visited the U.S. and toured the American Museum with Barnum. When they came upon Zip the astonished Prince turned to his host and asked "What is it?" – MICHAEL MITCHELL, *Monsters of the Gilded Age*

I give you Zip, *What-Is-It,*
pinhead, black, inexplicably adorned
with a pendant of George Washington,
in shaggy suit, gorilla-like,
putting up his dukes.
Across the grass
       (which close inspection reveals to be a rug)
a piebald black, the Leopard Boy,
whose singlet gapes to show his pinto skin,
The Negro turning White.
Zip has the upper hand.
Behind them could be clouds, or a volcano, and a path
that Zip is blocking. His furry arm repels
the other's stride. No advance
for the leopard boy, his fist in a white boxing glove
dragging Zip's dark shadow.

If you could fold this photograph in half,
you would discern the body of a butterfly,
each wing inscribed with text that flashes, beautifully,
the hard black rules that govern daily life.
The body is the hinge that swings the mirror,
the binding of the book that tells you
who you get to be. The photograph that shows you
what's not human. Zip and the Leopard Boy,
the Leopard Boy and Zip, two sides of the coin
I toss to you.

CHARLES EISENMANN LOOKS
AT A PHOTOGRAPH OF JULIA PASTRANA

What we can do with light. See,
here they've posed her by the stairs. This photo,
it's no good, for she is as she is. No art.
She's ugly, no? But we can make her uglier
with flowers, costumes, other ladies.
A thorn among the roses, as they say.
An image is an image, but a picture, it's a story
that tells us how to read, you get
the difference? They've tilted her head coyly,
and she looks down, eyes rising like a child's.
No good, no good. We need a woman
and an ape, the civil with the savage.
Put her in satin dress, descending a grand staircase:
clever satire of a most unlovely lady.
Put her with potted plants, decked out in paint and feathers:
from jungles hot and dark we bring the missing link.
Put her in sailor suit, arms crossed, leaned back against the wall:
the *frisson* of a woman in the costume of a man. You see?
She is not as she is. We make her tell a story.

Bring me those other plates. Just look at Krao.
Here she's a naked monkey curled in a tall man's lap,
and here the perfect princess, though quite hairy.
With Krao you need the clothes or else she's only monkey.
Or little Princess Lucy, two feet tall. See how the swing
she sits on shows her scale? That's art.
And here's the Lobster Boy. I made him
wear that suit, he thanked me for it later. The Dog-Faced Man
is just a dog without his velvet clothes.

The camera captures everything, the brightest light
and dark, the shaggy face and velvet, the woman
and the ape. See Julia, that ugly face atop a woman's body.
You can make her anything.

Imagine a picture of your sister or your daughter
and stretch it out. Do not stop pulling.
Stretch until the bones jut, until the body
reveals the frame. Stretch until all you see
are bones and eyes. This is a woman
who sends herself to sleep by counting ribs.
Rolls of quarters fit inside her hipbones.
Her elbows are as sharp as the corners of a mirror.
At night she dreams herself a feast.
The first dish is her thigh. The second her belly.
All day she devours herself.

Imagine a picture of your sister or your daughter
and crumple it. Fold until she is doubled,
tripled into herself. Continue until all you see
are the folds of her clothing. This is a woman
who wears many layers. Other people's voices
fit inside her mouth. When asked her name
she says nothing. At night she dreams
a flood and a throatful of water.
At night she dreams a fire and herself
burned away. She writes
     I am undead
     Mirrors do not show me
     And sunlight marks my skin.

Imagine a picture of your sister or your daughter
and tear it so many times
that the pieces become invisible.
Give them away to men you meet.

It does not matter whom. This is a woman
who needs men's hands to put her together.
At night she dreams herself naked on a stage.
In the orchestra there are one thousand mirrors.
All day she tries to remember her reflection.
All night she tries to reassemble herself.

ON LOOKING AT PHOTOS
OF CIVIL WAR WOUNDED

Truncated portrait of a black man, triple amputee,
a pail of feet, "A Morning's Work," a chorus line
of men, prosthetic legs insisting identically
towards the camera,

this is before anaesthetic, or penicillin, when every wound
turns septic, gangrene blooming in the skin's petals.
Nobody says *just a flesh wound*, pulls up his pants,
gets on with life, it is impossible

to get away from what machinery can do
to a body, the war's sentence repeating itself
in every empty sleeve.
Sometimes I think of torture. What it would take

to break me is less than you or I would think.
The question *yes or no?* above my wrist, my hand
a flower trembling with terror.

What could I confess?
The men went home to what was left
with what was left of them, smoke rising
from the ruined houses of their bodies.
A morning's work done

by three machines that shadowed them,
the gun, the saw, the camera,
their portraits saying yes and yes
and no and no and no.

The poet no longer knows he was a poet.
No words darken the rooms of his brain,
all is light, is sound, a thousand pictures
and no words.

At eight and four he gets pills and shots.
Later, something to help him rest.
He sleeps an old man's sleep, uncertain.
Dreams chase each other. Sometimes
he speaks, lucid, recalling names and faces,
when he was well-dressed and drunk by ten a.m.
He sought oblivion: now it seeks him.
Not the word, the thing and here he is
unlanguaged. Sees with clarity
the world for what it is: a train, a small
tin boat, a piece of paper, blank.

Though she turns alone at night
the still relief of sleep eludes her.
By day she walks across the floor as though
she has forgotten the way; as though
the kitchen is a place she had visited once
and cannot now remember.
Did she paint these walls?
Is this her handprint on the window?
There are some photos on the refrigerator
but she does not see herself in them.
Sometimes she runs outside, frightened,
turning to look at a house she doesn't know.

Something is missing or something is there.
There is no difference. When her children come
they tell her nothing has changed. She is still
the mother they came home to from school.
She says nothing. Her children open the fridge,
complain that she has nothing to eat.
She does not ask them who they are.

She wants to take out all the furniture,
all the pictures. She will take down the curtains.
She will lock the door.
Everything will be white. Everything will be new.
There will be nothing she does not remember.

ELEGY FOR JUMBO

"the pillar of a people's hope, the centre of a world's desire"
– EULOGY FOR JUMBO IN THE *Daily Mail* (1885)

Some say that Jumbo, drunk, charged the train
that killed him,
others say he threw a smaller elephant to safety
at the cost of his own life. Either way, he died,
his huge gray hide a screen that flickered
with the world's desires. Wedding cake,
whiskey, he ate whatever people gave him.
He showed up in advertisements
for toothpaste, thread, and soap, doing all his tricks.
Jumbo, made to carry all that we could want.
The pillars of his legs could barely hold it up.
He roared, got mad, got drunk. Perhaps
he watched the crowds, imagining them
monkeys peering through the bars of forest trees.
He must have wondered at the hats he wore,
the flags he waved. One time he ate
a small brass statue of a pig, no stranger, really,
than his daily fare. What his own desires were
none knew. He did what he was told
and so survived, imprinted with the wishes
of an empire.
            As Jumbo died,
his trunk sought out the hand of Matthew Scott, his keeper
and for twenty years his friend, and held it, private
world amid the blood and shouting. The circus stood
in swaying, jagged lantern light, apart.
Inside the thick container of his skin, he'd kept himself
a small and unseen land, unmapped, unadvertised.

Daily I protect the house, intercept
everything unworthy of you:
bills from credit cards, property
tax assessments, letters from
ungrateful offspring. These I chew
and swallow before regurgitating
beneath the peonies. You must not be disturbed
by cats, it is the least that I can do.
I pray you walk me. If I could burst this leash
I'd fetch you rotten apples, pee mightily
upon your stair. All hail! All hail!
The king is here, long live the king.

At four o'clock I dance on my short legs,
bark glyphic syllables to a fluorescent moon.
I pray, and dinner comes: kibbles
again. The joy. Yet I am a bad dog,
the kibbles rattle in my small tin dish.
I must be better, do all I can, I must
not gorge on garbage after supper.
Pray you do not know till later.
Soon, dog basket isolation,
my pillow cold. All night I watch your bed,
loathing my short legs. If I were better you would
love me more. You snore, oh growling symphony,
the hordes of thoughts I want to speak.
Did I not love you quite so desperately
I would kill you as you sleep.

TOBY, THE SAPIENT PIG, IGNORES
THE FLOWERS ON THE CARPET
AND REGARDS THE CARDS INSTEAD

On 'A' he muses apples, how his mouth wants
their crisp white bite, skin taut as his own belly.
'G' is for the grass he used to roll in.
For 'W,' his waistcoat, blue, with shiny buttons,
which he so likes to wear, and 'M'
is for his mother. For 'S' he thinks
of sun, and of his shiny buttons, and 'B'
is for the book he'll open soon.
And 'H' is handkerchief, and 'L' is letter,
both things that he will shortly gather,
and 'H' again is hour, which he will toll
by stamping. 'D' is for the dark.
For 'R' he thinks of roses, whose thorns
prick the inside of his mouth.
'Q' is quiet, quiet days, and 'F' is flags
that snap and whistle in the station.
'J' is for the joy that takes him, sudden,
all alone. And 'T' is for the thoughts
he will divine from 'C,' the crowd, who pay to sit
and gape and marvel at the antics of 'P',
himself.

TOBY, THE SAPIENT PIG,
THINKS OF HIS HEROES

Tschuschka, pig of strength,
     who braces all four feet and is surmounted by
          a rat, upon a cat, upon a dog, upon a goat,
            holding all the animals
               as Atlas holds the world;

Bill, the English pig,
     who stands upon one trotter
         on a sea-lion's nose,
            elegant, gymnastic,
               climbing out of gravity;

and nameless X, beloved pig,
     who is taught to shoot a pistol at a target,
         by a clown, his master;
            X practices and practices,

               wheels, and shoots the clown.

If you fall, your child will have fits;
if you spy through keyholes, your child will squint.
If you climb over carriage-shafts, your child will be bandy-legged.
Make water in a churchyard, and your child will be a bed-wetter.

If you eat speckled eggs, your daughter will be freckled;
climb under a rope and your son's cord will twist.
If you carry logs, your son's penis will be large.
If you see a mouse, your daughter will be marked.

Your son will steal if you climb through a window.
Your son will drink if you spill beer on your clothes.
Your daughter will be pale if you shroud a corpse.
Your daughter will hunger if you look into a grave.

If you're frightened by cats, your child will have paws.
If you dream of rabbits, you will deliver a rabbit.

THE STRANGE INCREDIBLE AND TRUE STORY
OF MARY TOFT OF GUILDFORD WHO IN 1726
AT AGE 25 WAS DELIVERED OF 17 RABBITS
UNTIL SHE WAS IN DUE COURSE REVEALED
WITH RABBIT 18 TO BE A FAKE FRAUD
AND CHARLATAN A VILE CHEAT AND IMPOSTER

I.

The day is dull
as potatoes.
I dig
the vegetable patch
one row
then another.
Twist spade
in sod.
Twist spade
in sod.
Sow last year's seeds.

All I want is a little beauty,
a little imagination,
the sky to lie in the millpond
so I can soak the clouds into my skirt.

You wouldn't hit a pregnant woman, I said.
He blacked my eyes, flattened
my belly. The day hangs
like wet cloth, like every other.
Nothing grows in the garden, nothing
flowers between my legs.
Rabbits root in the turnips, sodden, filthy.
Everything mud coloured.

When I lie on the floor with my head
in the corner I can see with one eye
things I never saw before. A spider's web
under the table. Clods of dirt
by the woodbox. A mouse, darting
quick as a snake. My other eye looks out
the window. The sky a faded blue ribbon
where clouds go by
clouds going by.

II.

A baby born with a pig's head, people say.

In Germany women vomit toads and frogs.
When they walk past ponds their stomachs croak,
people say.

A woman with a tail, she neighs
and gallops in the field.

People say and say.

III.

After the first rabbit, great jokes.
Feel my belly! See the conies jumping
as they rush towards the world!
These men so easy to fool. Moan, groan,
allow they might touch me themselves next time.
One doctor examines me
by standing between my knees as I thrash.
Another closely inspects my breasts.
Don't think I don't know what's under their shirts.
There's a line outside my door, rabbits
skinned and in my pocket.
Don't they want this to be true.

IV

When I was small I remember my mother
with an egg in her hand, it was lovely
and round and when she slipped it in the pan
it bloomed a flower white and gold.
One day a peddler with a great sack
said he'd carry me away. Would the sack
be like the egg, I wondered, would I fall out
when it opened, would I shrink to the size of a toy?

It is a crime to be a woman
who bears only babies.

I am a doll now in a house
that is a cell that is an egg.
You would blow me clean,

blank as the inside of a shell.
No matter how you shake the sack
I won't fall out.

QUESTION

All landscapes ask the same question in the same whisper: 'I am watching you -
are you watching yourself in me?' – LAWRENCE DURRELL

Tell me about the warmth brick gives off
in the evening of a sunny day, how shadows pull
animal shapes across your lawn. Tell me how
the delphinium's curve is the exact shade
of your dress. A small umbrella hangs
above your glass. Tell me the colour of your hair.

Your phone is quiet. Tell me who does not ring.
Leaves fan like a book tossed aside.
The open window admits it all: shouts,
sidewalk catcalls, the curving noise
of passing cars. What is the sound of your palm
held to your ear like a shell?

Tell me your favourite perfume.
The scent of your clothes after rain
describes the high green notes of trees.
Tell me where you sit, how a leaf's lip dips
across your vision. I want the geometry of your space.

Tell me how the leaves slip like a satin dress
over your hips, how animal shadows lick
salt from your skin. Your eyes push
pages through your palms.
Tell me where you think I am.

GRAVITY

You're halfway up the switchbacks, past bears and closed campground and bugs and shooting-stars and forget-me-nots and fireweed, past the stream that runs clear enough you forget the water's not safe to drink, halfway to where you'll make camp, the two of you alone (with bears and bugs) and no one else for miles and miles and miles but you and northern lights alone between the mountains, halfway when the ranger whistles you down and says someone you love is dead. She doesn't know who.

The grey rock beneath your boots yaws open, hard mountainsides shatter, the world cants wildly. Suddenly you understand gravity, the downward pull that is not persuasion but a violence that wrenches a thing suddenly from where it was and drops it somewhere else. There are still 18 kilometres between you and the parking lot. Your love's boot heels march ahead, they move on and on and your pack is so heavy now because you're carrying your family, they appear and appear though you try to see through them to boot heels and bears, your unstoppable mind calculating age and dividing that by illness and coming up with expendability while your body trudges on and on behind boots that won't stop moving and the mountain won't stop moving and goes uphill all the fucking way to the ranger station where you fight your way through the jungle of the radio phone to find out *what happened, over.*

And ahead of you again the boot heels trudge and trudge, grind grief and rage and pain into the oblivious sky, where it is impossible to locate comfort in speech because *I'm so very very sorry* also means *thank God it wasn't me.* The day is beautiful and you hate it, shooting-stars and bears and happy campers passing by with chirped hellos, you can't believe the mountains are still standing when a landslide's going on and ahead boot heels keep going down and down.

What comes of beauty:
the trout lurching in the boat-bottom
and night falling onto the boards

moving and lightless:
the fish, the fisher,
the net and the scales

DEATH SURPRISES ME LIKE MOUNTAINS

(in memory of Ray Cariou)

Death surprises me like mountains
in my new city, the suddenness
of them, turning a corner,

overwhelming
       like the earthquake they say is coming.

They say it's coming but no one believes it.
How else could people continue to live here?

The earthquake transforms
into headlines before it happens,
as mountains are transformed into postcards,
as Mt. St. Helens is transformed
into a National Geographic special,
no one remembering what it was like before.

Downtown one earthquake-proof building hangs
on improbable cables, touching the ground
at one impossibly balanced point.

Pay close attention:
after the earthquake there will be a new skyline.

PROCESS

If the human life span were a day, flowers might seem as enduring as rocks;
if we lived a thousand years, rock might seem mobile. – ANNE WHISTON SPIRN,
The Language of Landscape

Flowers, rocks. Here on Galiano Island
the cemetery is ringed by seals,
appraising us through sun-shocked waves.
Islanded, we walk through shadows
shifting under canopies of unreal trees.
Between their roots they cradle graves
planted deep in fertile ground.
The moving light evokes the dead:
curling ferns protect two red toy trucks,
a small clay dog atop a headstone.
Across the way, three photos and burnt candles.
And here, a plastic troll: fetishes
for the consumer age. Still,
there's power in glass beads, these tinny bells.
Giving something seems the thing to do,
I part the grass, leave quarters on a stone.
Shiny disks, to catch the living eye.

PROCESS (2)

Saskatchewan. More rocks.
Beneath a flashing radio tower
a dip in the Strawberry Hills cups a cemetery.
Six rows laid out neatly,
regular as furrows in a field.
Bleached crocuses and pale-eyed grasses
grow through dusty plastic carnations.
The wind tears our eyes, says *it's a hard one*,
seven gravestones marked only *baby*.
There's nothing I can leave here,
nothing that fits.

The night of your father's funeral
we walk the ditch beside the highway,
dust coating our mouths.
They are combining the field beside the house.
For days they have been getting closer, and
now they are here, a trio of ghost
lights crossing and recrossing the field.
They look like dinosaurs, something extinct
come back again. The red eyes of the grain trucks
blink in the distance, parked and waiting.
The air smells like exhaust, chaff, rank canola.
We walk between the highway and the field,
emptied, listening to machines.
On either side of us the ground shakes.

At midnight, too strung out to sleep,
we stand red-eyed in the yard to see
the trucks auger their loads into the bins.
It's good to get the crop off, good
to get things moving. The crickets sing
in the night, the dogs bark.
All night the trucks move
steadily past where we stand
trying to hold each other
in thin, shaking arms.

The dusty smell of my tread in the drying grasses, the sun angling through poplar trunks glowing like the gold leaf on a picture frame, every breeze-blown twig applauding the day; this is perfection. I think *if I were to die now I would be happy*, then think *no, not happy*, no more and no less than whatever creature's small bones lie white in the brown dust beside my boot, the small dreams of this place stilled in its clean and brittle skull. *Not happy*. But who's to say? The lake that flashes through the trees, the hush underfoot, the snapping fingers of the poplars don't cheer for me alone. Someone other than me saw that spill of sun. Inside that skull a voice may sound, immaculate collision of impression: dirt cool, sun warm, stomach on its way to being full. What pleasure in the grass, the hollow nest, bones not my own bleaching in the dust. What pleasure in the life that circles in my frame, electric as twigs snapping, slow as rocks heated by noon. *Happy? Why not?* I say to a blackbird, red wings flashing the colour of strawberry leaves under my feet. The bird flies away and I who am not dead but pleased anyway walk on, boot heels knocking the rocks from their places with quiet thuds heard by hundreds of unseen ears.

A "wolf" tree is a tree within a woods, its size and form, large trunk and horizontal branches, anomalous to the environs of slim-trunked trees with upright branches. It is a clue to the open field in which it once grew alone.
− ANNE WHISTON SPIRN, *The Language of Landscape*

The wolf tree's arms reach out
in a question that is also an answer,
as we seek another name for what we have.
The tree embraces us in its branches,
holds the buds of our tender dreams.
What happened, it says, what happened
to the farm grown over, the buildings
sagging into slope-shouldered grayness.
The wild comes back, as lilacs
explode over the woodshed,
irises and roses bloom beside
decaying doors.

The tree gestures, shrugging incomprehension
in a vanished field. Squirrels nest in a rusted-out car.
They've come back with the woods,
as the woods come back from the plough's perimeter,
as we come back from ourselves, rebounding
with what we thought was turned under and lost.
The grey farm died: farming killed it.
Poppies bloom in the wheat field, red
signals the rusty earth's exhaustion.
The hidden field is buried. The wolf tree reaches
among the slim and upright uniform trees,
branching left, right, toward us, away.

A STONE IS WORLDLESS
         — HEIDEGGER

A stone is worldless. Kick it
down a road, across the mirror
surface of a lake, until it sinks like,
well, a stone. John Cage composes:
freeze pebbles in a block of ice, suspend
above piano strings, wait for thaw.
Stone music. The dumb voice
speaks, a hammer and a key. Who listens?
The stone insensible
of falling could fall forever, it
makes no difference. The sound
of rocks clicking in a stream is only water.
In dark seams fossils move, rearrange themselves
in patterns. Look, they're still.

Open your fingers.
A pebble ringed like tree bark,
that pebble, a small world
falling.

ABNORMAL

Cancer, maybe.
Outlaw cells riding the range
of my frame. All the times
I wished my body were different..
Now it eats itself, my wish
come round again.

Outside this window
canker worms boil on a tree's bark,
a seething ball turning green leaves
to the gall of its own green swelling.

Rhododendrons burst from hot green,
magenta splashed on with a lavish brush.
Blooms hang, pregnant and tropical, petals wet
with the moist translucence of desire.
I'm heavy, dazed by the floral sheen
lustrous as bruised lipstick. I blush
at a blossom's damp folds. The flowers sweat.
And then, from this fire,

stillness. Underfoot, a nutshell consoles
with the sealed promise of what it contains.
Beside the path a maze of veins
resolves itself in the skeleton of a leaf.
Lucent, perfect: I think of our souls
and what they maintain. Love. Belief.

AS THE NIGHT IS SEEN
FROM INSIDE A CANYON

As the night is seen from inside a canyon, dark
ramparts cutting out a jagged bolt of sky,
constellations sparking between shadows,
so you look up to the night's glass, half empty
and half full, two faces and a vase;
the sky's cartography uncertain, so much
beauty or so little –
            so our love, mine,
is at once a presence and a loss, the hidden
larger always than the seen, which is so limitless
it surely must be all. And yet is not.
How can there be more stars when the sky has so much light?
A glass floats in a sea: our embrace
contains us in that hidden night, two faces facing.

Your muse is visiting. Again.
She's a bad guest,
demands attention at all hours.
She dirties the dishes
and never cleans a cup,
wears your clothes
and never does the wash.
She won't even give you time to buy the groceries.

Your muse won't stay in the guest room.
She hangs a *do not disturb* sign on your door.
Also, *please make up this room.*

Think a dog is bad?
Try making love
with a muse in the bed.

Your muse puts empty milk cartons
back in the fridge, leaves wet towels on the floor,
piles crockery in the sink.
While the two of you talk about art,
I wash her dirty sheets.

it could be a fish
it could be your foot
it could be true love's gleam in a golden ring
found in the belly of a salmon
it could be a leaf

will you open your eyes under water
to see everything truly
and all at once

if you want to see clearly you have to believe
you can   you have to duck your head and breathe
through logic and science and the terrific beating
of your small small heart

forgetting your dreams about drowning
forgetting those stories about girls
who walk on knives and lose their voices for love

green promises may lie under the water
you can swim and your eyes are open

the shore is not far away

TAJ MAHAL

In the city night a man builds the Taj Mahal
out of ice. His hands flash in the dark
as though he is dancing, signing
a language that transforms the word to glass.
Coloured lights glisten like tinsel
on a living room Christmas tree. The air
is full of stars, crystals, rings,
the kaleidoscopic glitter of a castle
in a paperweight. At the end
of the street, car lights sweep. Snow swallows
the sound.

This is a clear night, with frost. The moon
sculpts trees. Your footprints creak.
A man and his daughter walk the dog, stop
to talk at the Taj Mahal.
The words freeze in the air before them, hang.
The three of them lean together, laugh,
the dog licks snow in the coloured shadows.
The builder takes off his gloves.
Clear walls melt around his hand.

PORTA NIGRA
(THE BLACK GATE)

The black gate is really white,
but pollution and history have weighed it down.
There used to be a wall, too, around the city,
only bits of it are left. *History is everywhere,*
Martin tells me, *you can't dig a hole without unearthing
something.* It's true, I've seen the photos, Roman ruins
in someone's backyard.
There's even a perfume based on ancient Treverium,
the scent of a city,
whatever that's supposed to mean.

A little train takes tourists to see the sights in four languages.
In the cathedral I shadow a couple from Hamburg,
Ontario, eavesdrop on their tour guide. She speaks English.
All the historical periods are represented, she says,
look at the architecture, everything is here.
Next door, stained glass rises to the ceiling.
We walk looking up, bump into each other.

In the *landesmuseum*, black and white
photos of Nazis marching through
the Porta Nigra, their confident entry,
their welcome. I had forgotten this.
You'd think there would be darkness
marking these pastel streets,
these bland faces eating ice cream,
this corner where the spray paint artist
makes stars and moons to sell.
This beautiful flower stall in the middle of the market,
each blossom the centre of the city.

WOLSELEY

In the garden – a nice life
if you can get it –
catastrophic failure in the coneflowers, black rot
moving up the stems.
The lilies' sunny regiment folds like sniper victims.
Irises, past bloom, are holding strong for now, but underground,
who knows. Blight multiplies by air or water.
Still, the bees are flying, back and forth,
and back and forth, flower to hive to flower.
Like planes lined up on the flight path.
Like stitches pulled through fabric.
Like men who move all night long
through back alleys, rummage through each dumpster
looking for something, anything, to sell
or eat.

HORNET

Danger's in the smooth grey paper
hanging from the eaves, danger
in the muted whorls and crescents.
Hornets glisten black and white, shiny
as runner beans loosed from the pod. Don't touch.
Tiny jaws scrape the porch, then hornets launch themselves
towards the paper cave. Dark shadow of a door, round
as the spine's climb through vertebrae, as the tunnel leading
to the brain. The nest's a funnel cloud, growing
by the mouthful.

We'll wait for winter, do the broomstick thing, jump back
when chunks of shelter fall, dropping hornets.
Asleep, then dead. Their bodies punctuating snow.
In spring we'll turn them into earth.
Meantime, we watch the way they use our home
to make their own.
We watch them build.

Kittycorner from our yard: loonies,
but we say they're harmless.
The guy who stops before each sidewalk crack
to cross himself. The shufflers to the payphone.
The man who builds himself a belly
of things stuffed in his shirt. At 5 am
they're out on benches, blinking, having smokes.
Sunning themselves, slow turtles
with their meds. Sometimes they sit
all day. We cross the street though really
there's no need.

One entire summer, every night,
sirens cut the sleeping street awake.
From bed I read the noise: the start, the stop,
the start again. Slow glide round the corner,
then chopped off. Only lights.
Frequent flier says my brother,
the paramedic's term. An ambulance,
a stretcher, no one moving fast.
No one on the benches. Men shake
inside their apartments, hurting
no one but themselves.

From the tot lot, screams.
A balloon! No one's
ever been as happy as this baby
whose brother leans in, bonks her nose, leans back
again. She shrieks and reaches with closed eyes.
Each time she's hit
she scrunches up her face, then laughs like crazy.
again! again! And everybody's laughing,
the brother and the mother and me walking by
the bouncing balloon that's round and red
as her own red-hatted head.

Are there always hookers on your street
asks Gyllie, opening curtains.
So much for impressing out-of-towners.
Two weeks later we realize she's not *working*
the street, she's *walking* to work. On another street,
blocks north. Climbing into cars, going
down, turning herself inside out. Then walking home
along my street, swearing
at my neighbour's dog, buying herself a coke
at the corner store. Turning
her key, shutting her door. Then what?

VIMY

Vimy park oh you mean sniffer park

but that's no longer true. A change is coming
now they've cleared the drains. No shouting
in the night. No sniffing, or not much. Now, the fleshy blows we hear
announce communal drumming. Kiddies paddle in the pool.
Dogs chase balls, not people, and mostly not each other.
They know their names.
Apartment blocks get painted, turn up wearing bright new clothes
          called condos.
The shopping carts move west and north, metal rattling
on the jaws of sidewalks still split open.

Closer, potato plants burst through compost bins,
self-seeded poppies burn orange holes in flowerbeds:
something comes from nothing, all the time.
When we dug up the backyard we found iron,
rusted machines, an old rug. Discoveries
someone else had lost. And things recede.
Bittersweet that thrives two years
is lost to winterkill. Neighbours move away
in the night. Along the street a house burns down,
becomes an outlaw garden before it is rebuilt.
The edge keeps moving further, going somewhere
else. One corner of the park, away from where the construction is,
that corner won't stop sinking. They'll have to shore it up.
Whatever gets thrown in there disappears.

BASEMENT

The walls are scored with flood marks.
It is the elephant graveyard of good intentions,
the place where presents come
to die.
Drip-spout teapot, Santa shaped.
Squash racquet. Grad dress. High school trophies.
Dried flowers. Weights.
Sowbugs root among the canning.
Millipedes boil from mildewed cardboard.
Everything screams failure, failure.
We're not who we used to be.
We're not who others think we are.

Here our uncanny doubles are encoffined.
What would it take to kill them?
To drive that stake through dark, still-beating hearts?

Leaving the house last night I caught the stray cat
who lives under the compost bins next door
terrifying a mouse on the lawn. There was nothing I could do
and so I left, the cat's paw flattening the mouse,
one eye on me. Last summer I fed that cat and patted it
till she bit me, teeth scraping
the ridged bones on the back of my hand
like the claws of a hammer. Wounded.
Feral, that's what it means, biting the hand that feeds you.
Or *savage*, won't take what you want
to give. This was that kind of cat, malicious.
Quick burst of wanting her dead, then cold hostility:
no more kibbles under the porch. Why should I do anything
for what won't do anything for me? If it doesn't behave
I'll call the warden, will imagine its face
on every small corpse I find in the grass
as I push the mower on my green, green lawn.

who moved into the trunk of our car, overnight,
how we tried to get her out, and the three pink
pencil eraser babies clinging to her teats.
Little stowaways, messy cup-nest lined with foam
from god knows where. She ate the carpet in the back
and when we found her nest, she moved out of reach
inside the seat. She was too fast.
She chewed our map of Utah so the desert was a hole.
No going back. We drove.

Twice at night we saw her, frantic
in our flashlight beams she ran round and round our car.
Twice we saw her in the day, all eyes and ears,
the terrifying babies clinging.
Colorado, New Mexico: she wouldn't run away,
but held us, prisoners,
shreds of paper getting into everything.

And is it brave or not
to cast your lot with strangers,
and let yourself be carried?
Where does choice begin?
A mouse is not a metaphor.
It died in Arizona.
We learned exactly nothing
except how dead mice smell.
And yet, this mouse,
her tiny body turning
to a question. Who carries whom?
What can we say? Keep driving?

We hate the animals who live among us
as we hate our own reflections gone to seed.
Scabrous sparrows, shitting pigeons,
raccoons who strew our garbage on the lawn,
mice like bloated tampons in the well.
We hold them in contempt.
Squirrels cause fires: root them out,
destroy the nests they make beneath our eaves.
The blunted bears are at the dump tonight,
drive in to watch incinerator greed.
Destroy them too. They are not real,
not like us. We live, we fight for life,
we get and get and get. It's ours.
In darkness animals knock cans, chew bags,
spread trash as if we meant it to be seen.
They eat our trash, they are our trash,
they must be taken out and lost, like trash.
Oh how we hate the animals,
hate what we think we've made.

IMAGINING COMING HOME
AFTER YOUR DEATH

Mute blue folds of your dressing gown,
half empty cup on your side of our bed.
I think my way to this point
as the glass falls towards shattering
on the hearthstone. My heart
riven, your side no longer
mine. How could I not
light a newspaper, hold it to the floor
until the boards smolder?

Conflagration: to burn together.
A bright blanket unravelling,
erasing itself.

How do they live it, those people, bereft?
Coming home, beloved objects
speaking, speaking nothing,
mute.

TODAY

Each day is marked by small explosions:
plums lurk in the fruit basket,
violets burst into blue.

The moon, glimpsed, centres itself in a window pane.

The garden's shape changes
with the hang of the raspberry branch.
The dirt uncovers a small green bottle.
The cat sleeps in the window,
and today, the mailbox beside the front door
blooms: a letter from you.

I TRIED TO WRITE A LETTER
OF LONGING AND LOSS

Since you've been gone
I have lost seven pounds
and become reacquainted
with the piano.

Yesterday I watched
a three hour movie in Swedish
in which nothing happened.
I enjoyed it thoroughly.

The dog has slept on the bed
and I have peed with the bathroom door open.
I have started to paint
and am growing the hair on my legs.

As when standing in the garden, unmindful,
deadheading daylilies, my hand closes
on one more drawn and leathery bloom
that's past it, spent, a nuisance, nothing
more, but suddenly it vibrates, doorbell
against my palm, so that I peel
the petals back to find a bee —

the white cat dies, comes back to us
as ash and bone beneath the bergenias.
Where did he go? Because he went somewhere,
leaving behind what anyone would: dishes, toys,
his few belongings scattered on the floor.
Easy now to imagine the Egyptians, who also loved cats,
picturing their dead on journeys, burying them
with food, jewellery, things they'd need
as they rowed upstream to the future.
Dreams of consolation, the story going on
just like the soul. Easy also to imagine where
the small clean bones at the top of the urn-dust
fit into his plush body, slim pins holding
the folds of a soft, soft scarf. Here in our yard
we hold him in two hands, the urn at once
stripping him down to his essentials, no magic here,
just bones and physics and biology; but also this:
the sure and certain knowledge that he's shed
this skin the way a flower sheds its petals, shows
daylight to the bee.

The ridge comes back from the fire,
aspens twice my height, blueberry bushes
red blazes beneath willows. Here and there
spruce trees, small, fight their way to the sky.
They won't come back like before,
an inch of growth a year, aspens muscling
into the breach. Coming back
my tracks cross the tracks I made going out
and those I made yesterday, a grammar
of footprints. Action happening many times, never complete,
present imperfect. Process and progress.
Grief goes and comes back
like the dog who meanders on her own business,
appearing suddenly at the edge of the grass,
looping away, out of sight, until I look over my shoulder
and see her running, leaves thrown to each side.
Or she trots so close to my heels I can't see her
and call and call. Voice curving back from the ridge
after this ridge, the one after that.
That's what I did today, what I do, walk
my companion, measure trees, our own marks.

One day I hung out laundry, plastic clothesline scarred
and stretching under heavy sheets, but holding,
till as I finally turned away a bee buzzed up
and landed on the line.
It sat there for one second, then was gone,
the line snapped, clothespegs whistling past like bullets.
What we have to carry is more than we can carry.
The body bends around a blow, springs back
or falls. And still keeps going. *I'll never make it through,*
we say. One day my mother stooped to get a piece of paper
and her disc popped like a kernel in hot oil,
that fast.
Now she can't walk.
Beside her spine a steel rod keeps her moving.
You have to kill yourself, a student said, *take yourself apart*
and work your way around the missing pieces,
the way you take apart an engine,
or a poem. Technically,
flexibility is deformation under load,
your shoulders dragging the weight of grocery bags,
body curling in to shield itself as boxers will
when praying for the bell, enduring.
How far can I bend? What then?
I asked my mother once about her life.
She said *I've been blessed.*

SEXING THE PRAIRIE

How do you sex the prairie?
    The gopher was the model:
    Stand up straight:
    Pop in and out of holes.
    Vanish suddenly: the
    gopher was the model.
        – lines not found in Robert Kroetsch's *Seed Catalogue*

That prairie, she's a boy. John Palliser was a boy; so was Wallace Stegner. W.O. Mitchell was two or three boys. Even Sinclair Ross was a boy, but he didn't like it. Fred Grove was a boy too, but not here.

Let me tell you something about boys: Grain elevators. Telephone poles. Church steeples. False fronts. What goes up, must go up. Get the picture?

The railway? They don't call it "laying track" for nothing.

When these boys grew up they could take us girls out for a drink, escort us through the "Ladies & Escorts" door.

They could take us girls out. But they didn't.

Meanwhile, I was in the kitchen with a red-and-white checked dishtowel growing soapy and limp in my hands. My grandmother was up to her elbows in sinksuds and my aunts were packing leftover jellied salads into tupperware. The rainbow: orange jello with carrots and pineapple; green jello with fruit cocktail and maraschino cherries; pistachio pudding with dreamwhip and coconut. And vegetables. The jellied salads were all on beds of lettuce.

Back on the ranch, the boys were ranching. Riding their horses hard and puttin' 'em away wet. They thought they were pretty smart until they fell off their horses. Then they thought they were smarter.

When one boy fell off, he broke his leg. "That was the fault of this prairie," he said. "She broke my leg. I'll have to shoot her." And he did. That prairie was shot so full of holes you'd think a colony of nuclear-powered gophers had moved in.

"I had to do it," that boy said. "She was asking for it."

Things I learned about nature in the Fuchs Wildlife Exhibit,
Highway 16, Lloydminster:
  – what you can't shoot, trap
  – what you can't trap, poison
  – what you can't stuff, pickle
  – what you can't pickle, petrify
  – what you can't arrange in a natural, life-like setting,
dress up in little clothes and glue miniature decks of cards and
musical instruments to its paws What does this have to do with
sex? Got sawdust between your ears?

"We got to cover that prairie," said those boys. "We got to get her
covered."

They made up a shopping list: railways, towns, churches, brothels,
schools, ploughs, oxen, cows, horses, chickens, pigs, shotguns,
tractors, combines, augers, quonsets, fences, mail-order houses,
mail-order brides, crops, more crops, big trucks, smaller trucks,
medium trucks, pesticides, herbicides, gophercides, homicides,
genocides, indian agents, residential schools, mounties, the police,
ballcaps, cruise missiles, the KKK, Monsanto.

Here's what the prairie said: tornados, droughts, floods, hail,
thunderstorms, lightning strikes, blizzards, frostbite, isolation,
mosquitos, black flies, warbles, ringworm, leeches, prairie fires,
dust storms, blight, rust, pigweed, grasshoppers, gophers, magpies,
skunks, coyotes, more gophers.

Here's what I learned in the kitchen: Saskatchewan is a country of geometry. This prairie was built on the principle of the grid, or rather, the square. Lemon squares, chocolate squares, date, turtle, buttertart, vanilla dessert, cherry cheesecake, Betty's Best, chocolate chip, peanut butter-miniature marshmallow, brownie, graham cracker, grasshopper pie, Mildred's, Dora's, Ethel's, zucchini, carrot, banana, walnut, apple crumble, butterscotch, hawaiian, pumpkin, Shirley's died-and-gone-to-heaven squares. Baby squares, wedding squares, funeral squares. Square dances.

The square was the model. If you don't believe me, look out the plane window.

Those boys are crowding at the kitchen door, pushing each other forward and hanging back. "Come on in, boys," says my grandmother. "There's plenty of dishtowels for everyone."

But those boys aren't coming in. "Looks like work," they say. They'd rather be shootin' and hollerin' and having pissing contests over in the barn. They'd rather have a chaw and beat each other up, manly-like.

I sure wish they'd come on in. We could sit down right here at the kitchen table. We could look out the window, past my grandma's daylilies to the green and endless promise of the horizon. We could drink some coffee. We could have a real good talk.

HUNGER

to roll in sage
to smell of it

to tear it to pieces
to swallow the silvery air

to eat sage
to graze

to dig like a dog beside it
to have sage grow from me

AS THE BEAR STORES FOOD
TO STAY FAT THROUGH THE WINTER

a grouse's eye, ringed scarlet
orbit of a small dark planet

scandalous, northern laurel's
fuchsia bra with hiking boots

scattered cranberries floating
in a green pool, red stones

on a brook trout's back,
red circles closed with blue

brought close, the comma moon,
a white cat sniffing at the window

on the pantry shelf, dark
jars of rhubarb, raspberries

caragana blossoms, yellow
sails on a wine-dark sea

McDOUGAL CREEK

the fisherman leaves
and trout rise, discrete
throaty gulps specific as their names

whorls of their feeding
knots in burnished wood

trout sip

small worlds explode
move outward
catch
water iris nod
on the bank, cattails
shed their fur

water beads
the back of the muskrat,
a silver chain

blue flash
one damselfly
and then another,

      return, you

          see nothing.

I.

Blue-eyed grass, pale
and pretty, looking
so innocent,

sees what you're doing,
saw what you did.

II.

The stemless lady's slipper

> (pink,
> translucent,
> lightly veined,
> sparsely hairy,
> pendulous,
> globular,
> wrinkled)

looks exactly like
a scrotum

no use
pussyfooting
around.

SHE TEACHES HERSELF
TO CHOP WOOD BY READING POETRY

Aim for the point that everything circles.
There will be space to let you in.

At a certain moment a decision is irreversible, the weight
-ed blade dropping itself to impact.

You know people who've cut themselves
with their own axes.

Admire the pieces, how you can't put them together
to make a tree.

Thanksgiving. Highways full of cars.
Everyone goes or comes back,
everyone meets. We are on the edge of winter.
Geese fly south. Do they remember snow?
They fly from winter and it comes,
they carry it in their wings.
Can they feel cold follow, close as their own feathers?
They coat a slough like whitecaps,
ice and its own reflection.
They pile into fields, banked and windblown.

We honk the horn.
The geese reply. Sharp syllables
fall onto us, the geese
are their own storm.
Beyond the open window, stillness,
dust hangs behind the car.
We are pulling on the veil.
We breathe winter in and out.

Blue smoke in the field
is flax, hanging low and lovely on the earth.
Canola, sunglasses-bright, falls to ground in golden shouts.
Flax whispers itself, cerulean sibilance
a blue scarf sliding off
                              a dark woman's shoulders.
Not sky blue, nor the dugout's blue mouth,
not the mirage shimmering ahead on asphalt.
Flax
is utterly its own, blue
woven into the field's weft, pulling
the highway's thread over
                              the horizon.
The fates spin flax, kindling
flames for their shears.
Wrap yourself in this blue shawl,
this fluid drift of knit and purl.

THE ANIMALS DREAM

"What do geese dream of?
Of maize."
— SIGMUND FREUD

Inside his salty shelter the badger smells himself,
the entombed pharaoh reading hieroglyphic dreams.
Outside the snow piles up, fumbles at his door
but cannot move the stones.
The pharaoh sleeps.
The river under Faucette's field drips slowly,
when will the cup be filled and tip
to wash him with its waters?
He yearns towards the grubs, seductive
as the call from any Cairo market stall.
Their heat defies the barometric drop. He is beguiled.
But now, through dark, roots grow, ribs surround
his sleeping form. He groans, blunt-snouted,
noses at the webs that wrap him close,
his opiate stupor turning blue sky
to litmus red of poppies. He digs
his heavy head beneath his paws, cries out
for mother with her bursting teats.
And now the river's dry, the ferryman
returns him to the shore. He curls into his claws,
growls once to hear his voice. *I am*, he thinks,
I am, I am. And then he sleeps again.

WIND IN THE PINES

Wind in the pines sounds like traffic
and already I'm ashamed of my senses,
mistaking very air for mere mechanics.
How to make our way without direction.
Sisyphus rolls his rock, he's always at the top, we are
at that moment with him when breathing is believing.
Sisyphus knows things could go either way;
the torture's not the labour but the possibility.

The world is a good place. I believe this
like my grandmother continued to believe
the china dog her parents' parents brought from England
was priceless, though when she went abroad
she saw them row on row in Portobello junk shops.
Hope, flying in the face of proof.
How can you hope against hope? You have to
move to make a path.
I'll add my shoulder to that rock,
I'll take a china dog out for a stroll.

There will be no questions
about the relationship of fox
to rabbit, or rabbit
to fox. No questions
will be allowed at this time
or any other. The fox is
not in sight, nor is
the rabbit. Do not ask
what they are up to.
Yes, the rabbit is small
and frightened and you will
want to take it
home, yes
the fox is as red
as you think.
We will admit
that the rabbit has been known
to eat carrots
and that the fox has been seen
wearing trousers in children's books.
Do not ask if they have been seen
in the same place at different times,
do not ask what has been found.
This is history.
There is a rabbit and there is a fox.
We will take no questions about it, none.

NOTES TO THE POEMS

Zip (Untitled) – Zip, who was also known as the What-is-it, was the stage name of William Henry Johnson, an African-American from Brooklyn who was discovered by P.T. Barnum in 1859. Jackson, who suffered from microcephaly, was marketed as both a wild man (half-human, half-ape) and a pinhead. There is evidence to suggest that he was nowhere near as disabled as Barnum, Ringling, and other onlookers supposed, as indicated by his last words (italicized in the poem).

Plate no. 47 (Zip: Pinhead, c. 1885) – Zip and an unidentified "Leopard Boy" were photographed by Charles Eisenmann in 1885. The Leopard Boy likely suffered from vitiligo.

Charles Eisenmann looks at a photograph of Julia Pastrana – From 1876 to 1890, Charles Eisenmann photographed many dime museum and sideshow performers so that they could sell their likenesses to spectators. These *cartes de visites* were an important source of income for the performers and so they were carefully staged. Many of his photographs are collected in *Monsters of the Gilded Age: The Photographs of Charles Eisenmann* by Michael Mitchell. Julia Pastrana, billed as "The Ugliest Woman in the World" because of her hirsutism and simian-like features, would not have been one of his customers because she died in 1862.

Her likeness does exist in several photographs, and in many advertising posters. Like Julia Pastrana, Krao (1876-1926) was also excessively hairy and was marketed as "the Human Monkey" and "the Ape-Girl." Eisenmann photographed Princess Lucy Fisher in 1888, when she was 21. At the time of this particular sitting, she was 27 inches tall and weighed only 23 pounds. He photographed Fred Wilson, the Lobster Boy, in 1885, and Jo-Jo the Russian Dog Face Boy in 1884 and 1888.

On looking at photos of Civil War wounded – "A Morning's Work" is the title of an 1865 photograph by Reed Brockway Bontecou, MD. It shows a pail full of amputated feet.

Elegy for Jumbo – During his lifetime (c. 1860-1885), Jumbo was the largest Indian elephant in captivity and a source of fascination on both sides of the Atlantic. He died in St. Thomas, Ontario, after being hit by a train while on tour with one of P.T. Barnum's circuses.

Toby, the Sapient Pig, ignores the flowers on the carpet and regards the cards instead – Toby, a learned pig, performed in London from 1817 to around 1825. For part of his act, cards with letters and numbers on them were put on the floor so that, by pointing, he could spell out words and perform sums. He also gathered specific objects, told the time, and reported people's thoughts.

The strange incredible and true story of Mary Toth – In 1726, Mary Toth, a married woman living in Guildford, reported that she had given birth to a rabbit, and seemed likely to give birth to more. Investigation by several male doctors and midwives confirmed that she had indeed given birth to several skinned and dismembered rabbits. Other doctors were not convinced, and after giving birth to 17 rabbits Mary was brought to London to bear her next child under close supervision. After spending several days in confinement, being examined by an assortment of doctors, lechers, and hangers-on, she was caught attempting to bribe a servant to bring her a rabbit. When confronted, she confessed to her fraudulent behaviour and was imprisoned for some months. According to Jan Bondeson in *A Cabinet of Medical Curiosities*, "the prison was open to visitors and Mary was exhibited by her wardens like an animal in a cage." After her release, she returned home and little more is known of her.

Question – The quotation from Lawrence Durrell appears in his book *Spirit of Place* (New York: Marlowe and Company, 1969).

Wolseley is my home neighbourhood in Winnipeg. Classified as an inner city neighbourhood, it is also the city's granola belt, and currently undergoing gentrification.

ACKNOWLEDGEMENTS

I am particularly indebted to the following sources for inspiration and details for some of these poems: *The Feejee Mermaid and Other Essays in Natural and Unnatural History* and *A Cabinet of Medical Curiosities*, both by Jan Bondeson; and *The Language of Landscape* by Anne Whiston Spirn. Thanks to Yvonne Trainor for introducing me to Bondeson's writings.

An award from the University of Manitoba Faculty of Arts Endowment Fund partially subsidized my time at the Banff Centre Writing Studio.

I am especially grateful to Helen Humphreys and Don McKay, who read this manuscript in draft form and provided insightful and trenchant comments. Thanks particularly to Helen for the title. Roo Borson, Kim Maltman, and Catherine Hunter helped me to clarify individual poems. David Cuthbert also read and provided valuable commentary on some of the poems in this collection. I was lucky to work with Liz Philips, whose editorial eye and tactful commentary made reviewing this manuscript into an "aha!" experience for me. Thanks to Robin Gordon, Roewan Crowe, Vanessa Warne, and Dana Medoro for all the encouragement. Thanks to my parents for their unquestioning support. And thanks to Warren, for always making room in our house for two writers.

Selections from these poems were granted the Bronwen Wallace Memorial Award in 2004. A different selection received an honorable mention for the same award in 2002. An earlier version won an honourable mention in the Alfred G. Bailey manuscript competition. A number of the poems in this collection have previously appeared, sometimes in slightly different forms, in *Dandelion, Grain, Contemporary Verse 2, Prairie Fire, Xerography, The New Quarterly*, and *Open Letter*. Some poems have also been published in the anthologies *Breathing Fire, Exposed, 2000% Cracked Wheat*, and *Listening with the Ear of the Heart*. "Imagine a Picture" won *Dandelion*'s poetry contest, "Gravity (Garibaldi Park)" was a winner in *Grain*'s prose poem competition, and "The Animals Dream" placed in *Contemporary Verse 2*'s first 2-Day poem contest. "What comes of beauty" and "Today" circulated on Winnipeg city buses as part of the Manitoba Writers' Guild Poetry in Motion campaigns in 2002 and 2006.

ABOUT THE AUTHOR

Alison Calder not only won the Bronwen Wallace Memorial
Award in 2004, but was a finalist for the same award in 2002.
She has published poetry and prose in numerous Canadian
journals and anthologies, most notably *Breathing Fire: Canada's
New Poets* and *Exposed*. She's the editor of *Desire Never Leaves:
The Poetry of Tim Lilburn* and of a critical edition of Frederick
Philip Grove's 1925 novel *Settlers of the Marsh*.

Born in London, England, Alison Calder grew up in
Saskatoon and obtained her BA in English at the University
of Saskatchewan before completing Masters and PHD programs
at the University of Western Ontario. She currently teaches
Canadian literature and creative writing at the University
of Manitoba.